You and the Law Series

YOUR LEGAL GUIDE TO CONSUMER CREDIT

With a Special Section on Bankruptcy

American Bar Association
Public Education Division

Points of view or opinions in this publication are those of the author and do not necessarily represent the official position or policies of the American Bar Association or the Standing Committee on Public Education.

Library of Congress Number: 88-070394
ISBN Number: 0-89707-356-8

Produced by the ABA Press

Contents

Preface

Credit is a way of life in the United States, almost as American as apple pie. At any one time, about three-fifths of American families have installment debts outstanding—for cars, appliances, clothing and other purchases. Among these families, payments on their installment debts absorb about ten percent of family income.

Many families have mortgages, another form of debt. Mortgages are beyond the scope of this booklet, which deals with *consumer* credit—credit card purchases, cars bought on installment, etc.

Because the use of consumer credit has become such an important part of our lives, the American Bar Association has published this booklet to help you better understand how to use it, how to determine if you are reaching or have reached your credit-debt limit, and what to do if you have exceeded that limit.

The booklet will also help you better understand the federal rules, regulations and laws pertaining to consumer installment credit that are designed to protect you, the consumer. Additionally, this booklet will help you determine those situations in which the services of an attorney might be advisable.

Special Acknowledgments

We express our gratitude to TRW Information Systems Group, which has provided support for the printing of this booklet and enabled us to distribute far more copies than would otherwise be possible.

We are also grateful for the leadership and guidance of the U.S. Office of Consumer Affairs, which is directed by Virginia Knauer, Special Adviser to the President for Consumer Affairs. The Office of Consumer Affairs convened the group overseeing the project and offered expertise and support on all phases of the planning, production, and distribution of the booklet.

Acknowledgments

This booklet extensively revises and updates "Consumer Credit and Bankruptcy," an ABA booklet published in 1980. The revision is the work of Robert W. Johnson, Director of the Credit Research Center of Purdue University. Mr. Johnson's extensive knowledge of the topic and his skill as a writer enabled him to cover a complex area in a way that's understandable and helpful to the non-lawyer reader.

At the ABA it was edited by Charles White, Publications Director of the Public Education Division. Providing valuable assistance were Norman Gross, Director of the Division; Jane Koprowski, Publications Assistant; and Susan Filicchio, a law student extern from DePaul University College of Law. The booklet was reviewed by John Sheldon of the National Consumer Law Center and Vicki S. Porter, chairperson of the Debtor-Creditor Relations Committee of the Young Lawyers Section of the American Bar Association.

The booklet benefitted from the guidance of a group of experts on consumer credit and bankruptcy: Donald L. Badders and Mary Quinn, from the National Foundation for Consumer Credit; Elizabeth M. Doherty, Patricia Faley, and Robert F. Steeves, from the U.S. Office of Consumer Affairs; Steven Fier, from Associated Credit Bureau, Inc.; William J. Henderson, from the International Credit Association; Richard Sauer, Irene Vawter, and the Credit Division staff from the Federal Trade Commission; and Leo M. Spiekerman, from TRW Information Systems Group. We thank them all for their expertise and assistance.

An Introduction to Credit: What Is It? What Does It Cost? 1

Credit allows you to buy and use goods and services *now*, but to pay for them later. For example, credit lets you buy a car or a washing machine before you have fully paid for them. You can pay for them while using them. Of course, you could save to buy the car later on, but you may want, or need, the car now, not three years from now. Similarly, you can buy a pair of shoes or a dinner on your credit card now and pay for them later.

To consume now and delay payment beyond the next billing cycle, you usually must pay a finance charge, since you have the benefit of another person's money to pay the car dealer, appliance dealer, shoe store, or restaurant. Only you can decide whether it is worth that finance charge to have a car or other goods and services now rather than later.

As you will see below, the Truth in Lending Act (TILA) requires that all lenders (banks, department stores, credit card issuers, finance companies, and so on) provide you with information that will help you make that decision. For example, you may find that borrowing $4000 from your bank to buy a used car now may cost you the $4000 plus a finance charge at an annual percentage rate of 11% for three years. Is a "now car" worth it? If the term of your loan is three years (36 months), your monthly payment may be $131. Can you afford that? If you decide that the car is worth it and that you can afford it, you should then shop around for the best terms. For example, can you get a lower finance charge from other lenders?

The key consumer information provided by TILA is the annual percentage rate (APR). APR is an annual rate that relates the total finance charge to (a) the amount of credit that you receive and (b) the length of time you have to repay it. Think of the APR as a price per pound, like 20 cents a pound for potatoes. You may buy five pounds for $1.00 or ten pounds for $2.00. In either case the *rate* is 20 cents per pound (APR), but the total cost in dollars (finance charge) depends on the amount of potatoes purchased.

Let us illustrate the use of the APR in shopping for closed-end credit, that is, credit that has a fixed number and amount of monthly payments. Suppose that you're buying a $5,000 used car, putting $1,000 down and planning to borrow $4,000. How might you use the credit terms disclosed to select the best credit contract? Before you sign a loan, the lender must show you the amount financed ($4,000), length of loan, monthly payment, total finance charge and the APR.

Compare these four possible credit arrangements*:

	APR	Length of Loan	Monthly Payment	Total Finance Charge	Total Cost
Lender A	11%	3 years	$131	$ 714	$4,714
Lender B	11%	4 years	$103	$ 962	$4,962
Lender C	12%	4 years	$105	$1,056	$5,056
Lender D	12%	2 years	$188	$ 512	$4,512

Which loan offers the best terms? The answer depends partly on what you need. Clearly, the offer of Lender D is cheaper than that of lenders A, B, and C. Even though eleven percent is a lower rate than twelve percent, the shorter term of the loan results in a lower finance charge. However, if you are looking for a loan that would have the lowest monthly payments, then lender B offers the best loan. Only you can decide whether it is worth paying for two more year's worth of credit in order to lower your monthly payments. For an extra $450 ($962 instead of $512) you can cut each monthly payment by $85, from $188 to $103, but you will, of course, have 24 more of them.

In purchasing goods on credit, you may not be able to shop for credit effectively if you merely compare the APRs. For example, your car dealer may be pushing "incentive financing," by offering a 4.9 percent rate, while your credit union may be charging 12 percent on new car loans. In such cases, you need to find how much the dealer would charge for the car if you paid cash. By holding constant the down payment and the length of the loan from the dealer or credit union, you can see which arrangement

* Please note that these figures are correct even though the arithmetic appears to work out slightly different in some cases. Lenders frequently round off monthly payments to the nearest dollar, and adjust the final payment to make up the difference.

would give you the lowest monthly payment. In essence, you make all the terms of the two credit arrangements the same, except the monthly payment. Then favor the deal that gives you the lowest monthly payment to buy the car.

For example, a major automobile manufacturer recently offered consumers a choice of a cash rebate of $1,500 or 5.8 percent financing for four years on certain models. Assume that the car that you would like to buy under this offer costs $16,000, and that you have $2,000 for a down payment. You have the following choices:

1. Finance through the dealer. A $2,000 down payment, if required, would leave $14,000 to be financed over four years at 5.8 percent. Monthly payments would be $327.51.
2. Finance through a bank, credit union or other lender. With the $1,500 cash rebate and your $2,000, you have $3,500 to apply to the purchase price of $16,000. This leaves $12,500 to borrow [16,000 - 3,500 = 12,500]. If you can borrow $12,500 for four years at 11.17 percent, you will find that your monthly payments are $324.10.

This example illustrates the importance of checking all financing alternatives—and determining your bottom line payments—before making a decision. What is most attractive on its face isn't always the best deal.

A final point to consider when using consumer installment credit is whether or not the interest you pay is deductible when calculating your liability for federal income taxes. Whereas almost all homeowners can still deduct all of their mortgage interest for tax purposes, the interest that you may be paying on credit-card debt, student loans, auto loans and other debts is no longer wholly deductible. During 1988, only 40 percent is deductible, and the portion that is deductible declines to 20 percent in 1989, 10 percent in 1990, and 0 percent in 1991. When a line of credit on a credit card is secured by your home, the interest may or may not be deductible, depending on some rather complex rules. Since other previously deductible items, such as sales taxes, have either been eliminated or limited, most consumers will find that even the allowable interest and other deductions are unlikely to be as high as the standard deduction. Hence, in most cases, interest on consumer installment credit (not including mortgage interest) will not enable you to cut your tax bill.

Choosing a Credit Card 2

Open-end credit includes credit cards and overdraft checking accounts that allow you to write checks for more than your actual cash balance with the bank.

Open-end credit is increasingly popular in this country, as more and more people have credit cards. American Express, Diners Club, Discover, Visa and MasterCard are but a few of the many alternatives to choose from. How can you pick the card that's right for you? This chapter will look at some of the factors to keep in mind in making a choice.

The law helps you make comparisons between credit card options. Open-end lenders are required by law to tell you how they figure the finance charge you pay. The finance charge is always determined by applying the APR—which they are also bound by law to tell you—to the amount you owe (your "balance"). But the means by which lenders compute that balance differ so much that lenders who apply an identical APR can charge you very different finance charges, depending upon how you use the account and how they calculate the balance.

Alternative Ways of Figuring the Balance

Some lenders apply the APR to the *average daily balance* in your account over the billing period (usually about 30 days). Other lenders determine the balance by subtracting payments made or credits given during the billing period from the total amount you owe. This is called the *adjusted balance method*. Other lenders do not subtract from the balance any payments made during the billing period. This *previous-balance method* can cost you more than the other two methods. For example:

	Average Daily Balance	Adjusted Balance	Previous Balance
Monthly Interest Rate	1.5%	1.5%	1.5%
Previous Balance	$500	$500	$500
Payment (on 15th day)	$400	$400	$400
Interest Charge	$4.50 (average balance of $300 x 1.5%)	$1.50 ($100 x 1.5%)	$7.50 ($500 x 1.5%)

As you can see from the examples, finance charges may vary considerably depending on how they are calculated by the lender. In the first example, the average daily balance of $300, on which interest is owed, is arrived at by computing the difference between the $500 owed for half a month and the $100 [$500 minus $400] owed for the other half. In the adjusted balance method, interest is owed only on the amount you owe at the *end* of the period. Since you've paid $400, and thus only owe $100, you pay only the interest on the $100. In the previous balance method, you are charged interest on the amount owed at the *beginning* of the pay period—the entire $500.

Open-end lenders are also required by TILA to disclose whether or not you have a "free period" (or "free-ride period" or "grace period") and, if so, how long it is. The free period is the period between the end of the billing cycle and the date that you must pay the bill in full to avoid a finance charge. It is generally between 20 and 25 days. Some financial institutions do not provide a free period and levy a finance charge from the dates that your purchases, or borrowings, are posted to your account. This method of assessing finance charges is called the "true average daily balance method." Bank cardholders who take out cash advances almost invariably pay interest according to this method, and quite frequently pay a cash advance fee as well.

The free period may be modified under still another method of assessing monthly charges: the retroactive balance method. Under this system, you can avoid paying any finance charge by paying your bill *in full* within the free period. However, if you do not pay your bill in full, your next monthly bill will include a finance charge on the portion of purchases which were not paid for in full, calculated from the date those purchases were posted to your bill.

For example, assume that you bought a $500 item that was posted to your account on March 15. Say that you are billed on April 1 and must pay in full by April 20 to avoid a finance charge. If you are credited with a payment of only $200 on April 18, your next bill (say May 1) will include a finance charge on $500 for the period from March 15 to April 18, and then for the $300 balance remaining to the closing date for the May bill. If you do not pay your account in full within the free period in May, any additional purchases appearing on the May 1 bill will accrue finance charges from the date of purchase or the date of posting.

Other Charges

There are other terms to consider besides the APR and the free period when shopping for a credit card:

Annual fee. Credit cards issued by financial institutions often have an annual fee, say $15-$25, and perhaps $35-$60 if they are "premium cards" that provide you with a higher line of credit. In general, if you usually pay your credit card accounts in full each month (so that you don't expect to pay a finance charge), you should shop for a card with no or a low annual fee. In contrast, if you often don't pay in full each month, a low APR and a long free period may be more beneficial to you than a low annual fee.

Late fee. Most credit card issuers charge a late payment fee, say five percent of the amount past due, but not less than $1 or more than $5 per month.

Over-the-line fee. Some financial institutions charge a fee of perhaps $10 or $15 each time that you exceed your credit limit; that is, the maximum amount that the bank or thrift institution is willing to let you borrow at any one time. Usually the fee may be charged only once per billing cycle. If you plan to use your credit account frequently, you may find it necessary to keep close track of your outstanding balance, or to seek an account that does not charge this type of fee.

Variable-rate provisions. Some credit card issuers set APRs that vary with some interest rate index, such as the published market rates on three-year U.S. Treasury bills. These issuers must show you the index and the "spread," the percentage points added to the index to determine the rate you will pay. Also, they must show how frequently adjustments are to be made.

Some variable-rate credit card accounts provided by financial institutions can be secured by a mortgage on the cardholder's home. These accounts are called "home equity lines of credit" (HELC). Under a new federal law, lenders must limit the maximum lifetime interest rate increases on these accounts. Most lenders today set the lifetime cap at five or six percentage points above their current starting rate. Thus, if the starting rate is 12 percent, the lifetime cap would be 18 percent. Other lenders set the lifetime cap at a specific figure. For example, a large bank in New York offers an interest rate of just 1.4 percentage points above the bank's prime lending rate, with a lifetime cap of 25 percent (the New York usury limit).

How the Law Protects You—and How You Can Protect Yourself 3

TILA helps you choose credit wisely by requiring lenders to give you considerable information before you make a choice, but the law alone can't fully protect you—you have to cooperate by being an informed consumer.

TILA doesn't set interest rates; it doesn't tell you what rates are fair and what rates are unfair. Though 35 states set some upper limits on interest rates, rates in these states may vary widely below this ceiling. And that still leaves 15 states in which interest rates can legally soar to 50 percent or more.

It's true that the federal Truth in Lending Act applies to lenders everywhere, but remember that it only requires that the rate of interest—the APR—be clearly stated. As long as it is, the lender has complied with that law, even if the rate is sky-high and far higher than rates being offered elsewhere. So Truth in Lending is only a start. It provides assurance that you can have access to crucial information, but you must look for it—read the loan!—and compare it with rates and terms from other lenders.

Limits on Finance Rates

The shopping around you do for closed-end credit (installment loans) or open-end credit (revolving or credit card accounts) is a key factor in limiting and minimizing finance charges you have to pay. That's true even though most states also impose some rate ceilings (known as usury rates) on various lenders or types of credit. For example, the rates that finance companies may charge are frequently limited by state law, and a number of states also restrict the rates that retailers may charge citizens who hold their credit cards. But these maximums don't always apply across the board. For example, national banks may "export" their finance rates on credit cards. Thus, a national bank that issues cards from an office in South Dakota, which has no interest rate ceiling on bank cards, may charge cardholders in Iowa any rate it chooses, while all retailers selling to Iowa consumers cannot charge interest rates on their credit cards higher than Iowa law permits. In practice, it turns out that competition forces the national banks to keep their rates in line with those charged by state-chartered banks, other financial institutions and retailers. Note that in this example it is the pressures of the marketplace—the choices made by thousands of informed consumers—that set the rates, not the law.

If, however, you believe that a lender has charged you or tried to charge you a finance rate that might exceed a rate ceiling in your state, you should contact the office of your state's Attorney General.

What to Do if a Creditor Fails to Disclose Required Information: The Truth in Lending Act

If a lender fails to disclose information required under Truth in Lending, or gives you inaccurate information, or does not comply with the rules about credit cards, you should inform the proper federal enforcement agency (see pages 43-47). You may also bring a lawsuit for actual damages (any money loss you suffer). In addition, you can sue for twice the finance charge. The least a court may award you is $100 and the most is $1,000. If you win your lawsuit, you will also be entitled to court costs and attorneys' fees.

Truth in Lending originally applied to goods which were sold but did not apply to goods which were leased. Because of this, there is now a Consumer Leasing Act. With any lease of consumer goods for more than four months, this law requires the lessor (the owner of the property) to disclose the amount of each payment, the total amount you will pay, and whether there is a large (balloon) payment due at the end of the lease. You have the same rights to sue for violations of this act as under Truth in Lending, and you should report violations to the appropriate federal agency.

How to Apply for Credit 4

If you need to apply for credit, what factors may a lender consider in evaluating your creditworthiness?

Lenders generally look at:

1. Your ability to repay the debt—what your current job or income source is, how long you've worked or will receive that income, how much you earn; what your current expenses are: rent or mortgage payment, current credit payments, or average yearly family-related costs such as food, clothing, and school tuition.
2. Your credit history—how much money you owe, how often you borrow, whether you pay bills on time, and whether you live within your means.
3. Signs of stability—how long you have lived at your current or former address, how long you have been employed, whether you own a home or rent.
4. Your assets (car, home, etc.)—what can be used as collateral for your loan, and what sources you may have for repaying the debt other than income, such as savings or investments.

It is important for you to understand that lenders may use varying combinations of these factors to reach a decision on whether or not to extend you credit. But generally, if your credit history has been bad, your application for credit will be rejected.

Equal Credit Opportunity Act

Whatever credit standards lenders choose to follow, they are required by law to apply them fairly and impartially.

The Equal Credit Opportunity Act (ECOA) says that certain factors may not be used to discriminate against you in any part of a credit dealing. Basically, a lender may not use age, race, color, national origin, sex, marital status, religion, or receipt of public assistance to:

- discourage or prevent you from applying for a loan;
- refuse you a loan if you otherwise qualify;
- lend you money on terms different from those granted another person with similar risk (e.g., income, expenses, credit history and collateral); or
- give you less money than you applied for, if another person with similar risk would have received a larger amount.

The Equal Credit Opportunity Act does not, however, guarantee that you will receive credit. You must still meet the lender's standards of creditworthiness.

Age Discrimination

A lender may ask you your age, but if you're old enough to sign and be bound by contract (generally 18 to 21 depending on state law), a lender, by law, may not:

- refuse to give you credit or decrease your amount of credit just because of age;
- refuse to calculate your retirement income in rating your credit application;
- discontinue your credit account or require you to reapply for credit just because you have reached a certain age or have retired;
- refuse you credit or discontinue your account because credit life insurance or other credit-related insurance is not available to you because of your age.

The law does allow a lender to consider certain information related to age, such as how long your current income will continue or how long until you reach retirement age. For example, an older applicant may not be considered a good credit risk for a loan that will take a long time to pay back and for which adequate security is not provided. Further, a lender may take age into account in a valid credit scoring system. However, an applicant who is 62 years old or older must be treated at least as favorably as anyone who is under age 62.

Public Assistance

By law, if you receive Social Security or public assistance payments (such as Aid to Families with Dependent Children), you may not be denied credit for that reason alone. But lenders may consider certain information related to your income that has a direct bearing on your creditworthiness. For example, a lender may consider:

- the age of your dependents (you may lose federal benefits when they reach a certain age), and
- whether you will continue to meet residency requirements for receiving benefits.

Discrimination Against Women

Both men and women, by law, are protected from discrimination based on sex and marital status. Many of the Equal Credit Opportunity Act's provisions were designed to respond to charges of past discrimination that made it difficult for women to get credit.

The general rule is that you may not be denied credit just because of your sex or marital status (married, single, widowed, divorced or separated). Also:

- generally, a lender may not ask your sex on a credit application. (One exception is on a loan to buy or build a home. This is asked only because the federal government monitors housing discrimination and keeps track of female v. male house buying. You can refuse to answer the question.);
- generally, you do not have to use Miss, Mrs. or Ms. on a credit application. In some cases, lenders may ask whether you are married, unmarried, or separated, but only when that information relates to their right to obtain repayment;
- a lender may not ask about your birth control practices or whether you plan to have children; and
- you do not have to disclose child support or alimony payments to a lender. If, however, you choose to disclose this income, a lender must count it.

Marital Status and Separate Credit Accounts

If you are married and choose to open a credit account or take out a loan in your own name, rather than a joint account or loan with your spouse, a lender by law may not:

- refuse to open a credit account just because of your sex or marital status;
- require your spouse to cosign your account, unless you live in one of the community property states in which spouses are equally responsible for each other's debts; or
- inquire about your spouse or ex-spouse when you apply for credit based on your own income, unless that income is alimony, child support, or some type of separate maintenance payments from your spouse.

Change in Marital Status

If you marry or become widowed or divorced, a lender by law cannot require you to reapply for credit for that reason alone. A lender also may not close your account or change the terms of your account because you've had a change in marital status. There must be some indication that your creditworthiness has changed (i.e., your income is less). For example, if you are widowed or divorced a lender may ask you to reapply if you relied on your spouse's income to get credit in the first place. The lender must allow you to use the account while your reapplication is pending.

What to Do if Your Credit Application Is Denied

Under the Equal Credit Opportunity Act, you must be notified within 30 days after your application has been submitted whether your application has been approved or not. If you are denied credit, this notice must be in writing and it must list the specific reasons for denying credit or tell you how to request an explanation. The Fair Credit Reporting Act requires that the notice must also tell you if the credit denial was based in whole or in part on the use of a credit report, and, if so, you must be given the name and address of the credit bureau that provided the report. These same rights apply if an existing credit account is closed or an open line of credit is reduced.

If you are denied credit without explanation, first request that you be given an explanation in writing as required by law. If you believe you have been discriminated against, tell the lender why you think you've been discriminated against, and try to resolve the issue through negotiation. If the lender still refuses to extend you credit and hasn't given you a satisfactory explanation, contact a federal enforcement agency (see pages 43-47) or consult a lawyer for assistance. These same rights apply if an existing credit account is closed.

Under the Equal Credit Opportunity Act, if you think you can prove you have been discriminated against you may sue for actual damages (the actual loss you have suffered), plus punitive damages (a penalty assessed against the lender because the law has been violated) of up to $10,000 if the lender should have known that the law was being violated. If your lawsuit is successful, the court will award you both court costs and a reasonable amount for attorney's fees.

How to Establish a Credit Record and Check Your Credit Record 5

It may seem to many first-time borrowers that in order to get credit you have to have credit. There are many ways you can begin to build up a good, solid credit history. For example, you can:

- open a checking or savings account, or both—many lenders may turn to these accounts to establish that you have money and know how to manage it.
- apply for a local department store credit card— lenders can turn to these accounts to establish that you repay your bills on time.
- deposit an amount in a bank, savings and loan association or savings bank and borrow against it.
- get someone to cosign the loan with you (the person will be responsible for the debt if you can't pay), thus securing your first loan on the basis of someone else's credit. After the loan is repaid, you will find it easier to secure credit on your own.

Spouses should establish credit records in their own names while still married, especially if they do not earn wages. Many do not do this. When the non-earning spouse is divorced or widowed, and does not have an established credit history separate from the former spouse, the Equal Credit Opportunity Act requires lenders to consider the credit history of any accounts held jointly with the former spouse. Lenders also are required to look at the credit record of any account held only in the former spouse's name if the non-earning spouse can show with checks, receipts or other records that it also reflects his or her own creditworthiness. Likewise, if the former spouse's credit record is unfavorable, the non-earning spouse may show that the record does not reflect his or her own creditworthiness by producing previous explanatory letters sent to lenders, copies of contracts signed solely by the spouse, receipts or other evidence.

Many prospective lenders today turn to records kept by consumer credit reporting agencies, also referred to as credit bureaus, when you apply for a loan or credit. There may be a number of credit bureaus operating in your area with essentially the same information about you. Nationwide credit bureaus maintain computer files of financial payment histories, public record data, and personal identifying data and provide copies to authorized credit grantors. Credit information may also be sought when you apply for insurance, employment, etc.

Credit bureaus do not make credit decisions; they provide information to credit grantors so that the credit grantor may make credit decisions. Credit bureaus are authorized by law to disclose credit information from their files to any person or organization with a legitimate business need for the information in connection with a transaction involving the consumer. You have the right to examine your own file, and many experts suggest regular credit record check-ups to enable you to find out what the credit bureaus have in your file (and thus what they report to those seeking information about your credit record). If you are interested in reviewing your file, the Fair Credit Reporting Act allows you to do so at any time. The credit bureau may charge you a reasonable fee for providing this service, generally less than $20.

As noted earlier, if a prospective lender turns you down because of unfavorable information in a credit report from a credit bureau or agency, the law requires that the lender provide you with the name and address of the agency that furnished the report. You may request a disclosure from the credit bureau by phone, mail or in person. Although under federal law you are not entitled to receive an exact copy of your credit file, many credit bureaus will provide you with a copy. If you don't get a copy of your credit file, you will at least receive an oral summary of it. The law also requires the credit bureau to tell you where it got its information, except for information used solely in investigative reports, and to identify everyone who has received a copy of the report in the last six months (two years for employment reports). The credit bureau must also help you interpret the data. If you have been refused credit within the past 30 days because of information furnished by a credit bureau, the bureau cannot charge a fee for giving you information—you are entitled to receive a disclosure of your report at no charge.

If you find that the credit report contains inaccurate, incomplete or obsolete data, you have the right to challenge the accuracy or completeness of any item of information, and the credit bureau must either verify its information within a reasonable period of time or delete it from its files, unless it has reason to believe the dispute is frivolous or irrelevant. If you disagree with the determination of the credit bureau, you have a right to challenge their decision in court.

If the bureau finds that its information is incorrect, it must correct its report. Any information that cannot be verified must be deleted. Most adverse information more than seven years old, including suits, court judgments and tax liens, may not be included in consumer credit reports, unless such reports are furnished in connection with a credit or life insurance transaction involving a principal amount of $50,000 or more or employment at an annual salary of $20,000 or more. There is an exception to this rule for bankruptcies, which may be reported for ten years.

If the credit bureau's reinvestigation of an item you dispute does not resolve the matter, you may file your version of the story in a brief statement (100 words or less), and the credit bureau must include your statement, or a clear and accurate codification or summary of it, in all future reports containing the disputed item. You may also request that the credit bureau mail copies of your statement to anyone who has received a report containing the disputed item during the last six months (two years for employment reports).

Under the Fair Credit Reporting Act, you may bring a lawsuit against any credit reporting agency or lender who violates any provisions of the Act, including any credit reporting agency that fails to observe the requirements about who may have access to your credit records, or any credit reporting agency that does not properly correct inaccurate information in your file that you have disputed. However, if the agency has followed reasonable procedures, it has fulfilled the mandate of the law. But if your lawsuit is successful, you are entitled to actual damages, plus punitive damages if you can prove the violation was intentional. If you are successful you will also receive court costs and a reasonable amount for attorneys' fees. Any unauthorized person who secures a credit report under false pretenses, or any employee of a credit reporting agency who knowingly and willfully supplies a credit report to unauthorized persons, may be fined up to $5,000 or imprisoned for one year, or both.

You may also see "credit repair clinics" advertised. These clinics can help you review and update your credit record and report, but fees could range as high as $1,200. Remember, if there is an error in your credit report, you can correct it yourself at no cost or at very low cost. If a credit repair clinic promises or guarantees that accurate records of bankruptcy and bad debts can be taken off your credit record, be very suspicious and careful. Generally, if you are offered a credit program that sounds too good to be true, it probably is.

How to Correct Credit Mistakes 6

Once you have established credit, the best way to keep in good standing is to repay your debts on time. But what happens if you discover an error on your bill, or discover that goods bought on credit are damaged or defective? What option do you have besides not paying for these goods, which is then reported and hurts your credit rating?

Billing Errors

The Fair Credit Billing Act requires lenders to correct errors promptly, without any damage to your credit rating. Under the law, a billing error is defined as a charge:

- for something you didn't buy, or for a purchase made by someone not authorized to use your account;
- that is not properly identified on your bill, or is for an amount different from the actual purchase price; or
- for something that you refused to accept on delivery or that was not delivered according to agreement.

Billing errors may also include:

- errors in arithmetic;
- failure to reflect a payment or other credit to your account;
- failure to mail the billing statement to your current address, provided the lender received notice of that address at least 20 days before the end of the billing period; or
- an item for which you request additional clarification (a potential error).

If you think your bill is incorrect, or if you simply want more information about it, take the following steps:

1. Notify your lender in writing so the lender receives the notice within 60 days after the bill was mailed. Your letter must be sent to the address your lender has supplied for this purpose. *A phone call will not preserve your rights* if your lender has given you an address to write to.
2. In the letter tell the lender your name, address and account number and that you believe your bill contains an error—specify the error, why you believe it is wrong, the date and the suspected amount of the error.

It is important to know that *most* companies today provide a customer with a sales slip only at the time of purchase, not with the monthly statement. Under this billing procedure, the statement will generally give the date and amount of purchase, and perhaps the store and department in which it was made. It is therefore essential to keep all sales slips so that you can check them against the monthly billing statements.

The lender is required by law to acknowledge your letter within 30 days, unless the billing error can be corrected in less time. Your account must be corrected within two billing periods (in no case longer than 90 days from the time the lender receives notice of your dispute), or the lender must tell you why the lender believes the bill is not in error.

If no error is found, the lender, by law, must promptly send you a statement of what you owe. The lender may include any finance charges that have accumulated and any minimum payments you missed while you questioned the bill.

If, in fact, your bill does contain an error, you do not have to pay any finance charges on the amount in dispute or any minimum payments or finance charges that apply to it.

A lender may not threaten your credit rating because you fail to pay the disputed amount or related finance or other charges while you're in the process of resolving a billing dispute. Once you have taken the steps described above by putting your credit question into writing and sending it to your lender, the lender is prohibited from telling other lenders or credit bureaus that you have failed to pay the disputed amount or related finance or other charges. Until the lender answers your complaint, the lender is prohibited from taking any action to collect the amount in dispute.

However, after the lender has explained your bill, the lender may take action to collect if you do not pay in the time allowed, and the lender may report you to the credit bureau as delinquent on the amount in question.

If this happens, you may still disagree with the lender in writing. If you choose to do this, the lender must report to the credit bureau that you have challenged the bill, and the lender must give you written notice of the name and address of each person who has received information about your account.

When the dispute is eventually settled, the lender must promptly contact each person who has received information about your account and report the outcome.

If the lender doesn't follow all the rules within the proper time limits, the lender cannot collect the first $50 of the amount in dispute between you, even if it is money you do owe.

Defective Goods or Services

If you use a store credit card to purchase goods that are shoddy or damaged or receive poor quality services purchased with a store credit card, the Fair Credit Billing Act can help. The Act provides that you may withhold payment for the disputed transaction at the time you first notify the merchant of your claim or defense, so long as you have made a *real* attempt to solve the problem with the merchant.

If you purchased the goods or services with a bank, travel or entertainment card, or any other card not issued by the store where you made your purchase, you must still make a real attempt to solve the problem with the merchant and the right of withholding payment is limited to purchases totaling more than $50 that took place in your home state or within 100 miles of your home address.

If you refuse to pay because the goods or services were defective, your lender might sue you for payment. If this happens, the defective nature of the goods or services can be raised and if found valid is a defense to that suit.

Lost or Stolen Credit Cards

Your liability on lost or stolen credit cards is limited under the Truth in Lending Act.

It is very important that you notify the credit card company as soon as you notice the loss or theft of your card or cards—you do not have to pay any unauthorized charge made after you notify the company. The most you will have to pay, however, for any unauthorized charges is $50 on each card—regardless of how high the total run up before you report your card missing.

Under the Truth in Lending Act, a card company also may not collect any loss from you—even the first $50—unless they can prove the following four things:

1. that they issued you the card at your request or that the card was issued as a renewal or substitute for an accepted card, or that you used it at least once before it was lost or stolen;
2. that they provided some means on the card, such as a signature line, to identify you as the person authorized to use it;
3. that they notified you of your potential $50 liability; and

4. that they notified you that you may give oral or written notification that the card was lost or stolen and that they describe a means of notification (for example, a telephone number, an address, or both).

It is a good idea to keep a list of all your credit cards, the account number on each card, and the means of notifying credit card issuers of lost cards. Since you are most likely to lose credit cards when traveling, always take a copy of the list with you, keeping the list separate from your credit cards. Then, if your cards are lost or stolen, you will not forget to notify any of your lenders.

How Much Credit Can You Handle? 7

There is no general, all-encompassing way to determine how much credit you can handle. However, one long-standing rule is that if your monthly payments on debts, excluding your home mortgage payment, exceeds 20 percent of your after-tax or take-home pay, you most likely have reached your credit-debt limit. Or to put it another way, a roughly equivalent credit-debt limit for all installment credit payments is 30 percent of your pretax income. Since less than three percent of American families find themselves with installment payments at 30 percent or more of their gross income, you can see that relatively few families permit their debt burdens to reach beyond that limit.

Other indications that you are heading toward or have already reached your credit-debt limit are any of the following:

- you are making only minimum payments on your monthly credit accounts;
- you have to use credit for expenses that you once paid cash for;
- you have used a series of consolidation loans or other types of loans in an effort to pay overdue bills;
- you find it difficult if not impossible to save even small amounts;
- you have more and more trouble each month stretching your budget to make ends meet.
- you are borrowing from one lender to pay another; e.g., you take a cash advance on your bank card to pay amounts owed other banks or retailers.
- you begin to run a few days late on critical payments, such as your rent or mortgage payment, or you are consistently late with all your bill payments.

- you rely on working overtime, or on a second job, to pay bills.
- you are denied credit.

If the above describes your current state of affairs, you have probably exceeded your credit-debt limit.

Most experts agree that the first thing you should do is slow down or even stop taking on more debts. Second, examine your budget and see if there are any places where you can cut spending, so you can free more money to meet your monthly bills.

In some cases you may want to approach one or more of your lenders and try either to reduce or defer monthly payments without having to pay a penalty. Simply be honest in explaining your cash flow problem and ask the lenders if they can help you get back on your feet. While there is no guarantee that lenders will agree to this arrangement, the worst thing that you can do is to try to avoid the lenders or to make promises to pay that you don't keep.

In more extreme cases, you may want to contact a credit union or consumer credit counseling service that can help you set up a new budget (see page 47).

If you're having financial difficulties and become delinquent in paying your bills, lenders have rights under state law to try to obtain payment. As noted earlier, they are very likely to report your delinquencies to one or more credit bureaus, thus jeopardizing your credit rating. In many states they may seek a judgment and court order to garnish your wages; that is, an order to your employer to pay directly to the lender some portion of your wages. For a car, truck, home appliance or other durable good purchased on credit, your lender probably has a lien on the item that you purchased for the balance of the loan. Having a lien means that, if you fail to pay as agreed, the lender may recover (repossess) the item that you purchased on credit. Many state laws require that lenders notify you, say two weeks in advance, of their intent to repossess so that you have a last chance to pay your outstanding debt on the item. (Most agreements specify that when you are in default, the *entire loan* is immediately due.) Nor does repossession of your car, for example, end your obligation to the lender. If your unpaid balance and accumulated, unpaid finance charges, plus the lender's costs of repossessing the car, are less than the net amount that the lender obtains from the sale of the car, you are still legally liable to the lender for the shortage.

Whatever your financial condition, here is one simple way to determine your credit ceiling. First, total your *monthly* income:

Your take-home pay	________________
Spouse's take-home pay	________________

Other income	________
	________
	________
A. Total	________

Next, total your *monthly* expenditures:

Food	________
Rent or mortgage payments	________
Utilities	________
Telephone	________
Insurance (car, life, medical, other)	________
Car expenses	________
Other	________
	________
	________
B. Total	________

Next, total monthly payments on all of your current debts:

Personal loans	________
Charge accounts and other credit payments	________
	________
	________
C. Total	________

Next, total your *annual* expenses:

Taxes	________
Insurance (not paid monthly)	________
Medical and dental bills	________
School costs	________
Clothing	________
Entertainment	________

Vacation	__________
Other	__________
	__________
	__________
Annual Total	__________
D. Monthly Total (divide by 12)	__________
E. Monthly income available for savings or credit payments: A–B–C–D = E	__________

This calculation gives you the maximum amount that is available to you. These funds could be used for new credit spending or for savings. A rule of thumb is that an emergency fund in the form of savings or other readily accessible assets should equal three to five months of after-tax income. That means that if your after-tax income is $1000 per month, you should have from $3000 to $5000 available in savings or in another form that could easily be converted into cash.

Many people find that they can save more readily if they treat savings as a debt that they owe to themselves, so that each month, as they pay their other bills, they pay a set amount to their savings program. Some employers provide this service, automatically depositing a portion of your salary to a savings program.

Debt Collection and the Law 8

If, for whatever reason, you are unable to meet your financial obligations, you may come in contact with a debt collector or a debt collection agency. The Fair Debt Collection Practices Act, a federal law, prohibits abusive, deceptive and unfair debt collection practices by debt collectors. The primary purpose of this law is to see that people are treated fairly by debt collectors.

Key Questions

Who is a debt collector? Under the law, a debt collector is someone, other than a lender, who regularly collects debts for others. (There are a few minor exceptions to this definition.) Lenders are not covered by the federal law, but their collection practices are likely to be governed by laws in your state. The provisions of these laws are generally similar to those of the federal Fair Debt Collection Practices Act.

How Can a Debt Collector Contact You? A debt collector may contact you by mail, or in person or by telephone or telegram during convenient daytime hours. A debt collector may not contact you at inconvenient or unusual times or places, such as before 8:00 a.m. or after 9:00 p.m., unless you agree. Also, a debt collector cannot contact you at work if your employer disapproves.

How Can You Stop a Debt Collector from Contacting You? You may notify a debt collector by mail not to contact you. Once you tell a debt collector in writing not to contact you, the debt collector can no longer do so, except to tell you that there will be no further contact or to notify you that some specific legal or other action may be taken, but only if the debt collector actually plans to take such action.

Debt collectors must also discontinue efforts to contact you if you notify them by mail within thirty days after you are first contacted that you dispute the debt or some portion of it. However, a debt collector can begin collection activities again if you are sent proof of the debt, such as a copy of the bill.

What Is the Debt Collector Required to Tell You about Your Debt? Within five days of an initial contact, a debt collector must send you a written notice telling you:

- the amount of money you owe;
- the name of the lender to whom you owe the money;
- that the debt collector will assume the debt is valid unless a consumer disputes it within thirty days; and
- what to do if you believe you do not owe the money.

Whom Can a Debt Collector Contact Concerning Your Debt? A debt collector may contact any person to locate you. However, in the location effort, the debt collector cannot, in most cases, talk to any person more than once or refer to the debt in any way when talking to such persons. If debt collectors are using the mails to contact you or another person, they may not send letters in envelopes identifying themselves as bill collectors, nor may they send a postcard. Once collectors are aware or notified that you are represented by an attorney, they may communicate only with your attorney.

What Types of Debt Collection Practices are Prohibited? A debt collector may not harass, oppress or abuse any person. For example, a debt collector cannot:

- use threats of violence to harm you, your property or reputation;
- use obscene or profane language;
- repeatedly use the telephone to annoy you;
- make you accept collect calls or pay for telegrams;
- advertise your debt.

A debt collector may not use false statements when attempting to collect a debt. For example, a debt collector cannot:

- misrepresent the amount of the debt;
- falsely imply that the debt collector is an attorney;
- tell you that you will be arrested or imprisoned if you do not pay your debt, unless this is legally possible and the debt collector or the lender fully intends to do so;
- tell you that your property or wages will be seized, garnished, attached or sold unless the debt collector or the lender intends to do so and it is legal.

What Can You Do if the Debt Collector Breaks the Law? If debt collectors violate any portion of the Fair Debt Collection Practices Act, you have the right to sue them in a state or federal court within one year from the date the law was violated. You may recover money for the actual damage you suffered in addition to an amount up to $1,000 for an individual and up to $500,000 in a class action suit—a suit brought by a group of individuals who claim that they all have been injured (that is, injured as a class) by the illegal debt collection practice. You may also recover court costs and attorneys' fees. However, consumers found acting in bad faith against a debt collector can be held liable for court costs.

You should also contact and file a complaint with the proper federal government enforcement agency (see page 43). Many states also have debt collection laws of their own. Check with your state Attorney General's office to determine your rights under state law.

Deep in Debt: Bankruptcy and Other Alternatives 9

Being in over your head financially is a frightening experience. If you find yourself in this unhappy position, several kinds of help are available. You need to examine the options available to you and decide which course of action is in your best interest.

Some individuals in financial trouble can improve their situation by negotiating with lenders, others are helped by a financial counseling program with experience in negotiating with lenders and in budgeting plans. And for some, a form of bankruptcy may be the only realistic alternative.

If you find yourself in financial trouble serious enough to be considering these options, you should probably seek advice from a lawyer who is familiar with the bankruptcy laws. The choice of remedy isn't easy, and a lawyer or a financial expert in a credit union, bank, or similar institution can best advise you about the most appropriate solution to your financial problems.

Alternatives to Bankruptcy

There are alternatives which can be used to take care of debts which you cannot pay at this time. Lenders may be willing to compromise their claim for a smaller cash payment. Or they may be willing to stretch the payments out, so that you can pay the debt off by making smaller payments over a longer period of time.

If the lender is a retailer, you probably should contact the credit manager. If the lender is a bank which has issued you a credit card, you should contact the credit card manager. If your accounts are past due, with either a credit card company or a retailer, you should contact the person in charge of collections.

If you have a number of lenders, you may contact them individually and ask them to agree to a voluntary plan for the payment of their debts. The problem with this approach is that a lender may be unwilling to give you more time without knowing what other lenders are willing to do. If you owe only a few lenders, perhaps you could arrange a joint meeting with all of them to discuss a plan that would enable you to pay off your debts over time.

If you are having problems paying your bills and need help, another option is a financial counseling program. Some universities, local courts, extension agents, military bases, credit unions, housing authorities and banks operate such programs and charge little if anything for their assistance.

Under repayment plans set up by some financial counseling programs, you may pay the program a certain amount each month, which is then distributed among lenders until they are all paid in full. In addition, there may be a small monthly service fee. However, most of the support for financial counseling services is provided by lenders, who agree to allocate to them a portion of your monthly payments. Most lenders would prefer that you use this kind of plan (since they will eventually get most of their money) rather than "straight" (Chapter 7) bankruptcy. Under a repayment plan through a financial counseling service, you may still pay interest charges on your debts, but a number of lenders will waive interest charges and delinquency fees once you have agreed to repay your debts through a financial counseling service.

There are nonprofit and for-profit financial counseling centers. Nonprofits get most of their fees from lenders and hence the costs to you may be lower than for-profit centers. However, some believe that this may raise some conflicts by favoring arrangements advantagious to lenders. While many for-profit lenders provide worthwhile services, some may exaggerate the benefits that they promise. As usual, it pays to be an informed consumer. Shop around and check carefully before you decide on a center.

What Is Bankruptcy?

Individuals and businesses sometimes cannot pay their debts when they become due. The bankruptcy laws permit them to ask a court to find them officially unable to meet their debts. If their petition to the court is granted, their estate is then administered for the benefit of their lenders. This process is known as "declaring bankruptcy."

Bankruptcy laws exist for the benefit and relief of both lenders and borrowers. On the one hand, bankruptcy laws provide an orderly process for dividing the borrower's property and repaying each lender on as full a basis as possible. On the other hand, the laws are intended to give borrowers a fresh start in rebuilding their economic lives.

There are a number of specific parts, or chapters, of the federal bankruptcy law, and these offer alternatives to debtors. Chapter 11 of the federal bankruptcy act is generally not intended for consumer borrowers because of the expense and complexity of the proceedings. Consumer borrowers typically utilize Chapter 7 or 13. Proceedings under Chapter 7 (straight bankruptcy) involve taking a portion of the borrower's property (nonexempt assets, as explained later) and distributing it among his or her lenders. Bankruptcy plans under Chapter 13 typically extend the time for repayment, but involve repaying a portion of the debt in installments from the borrower's income. Under any chapter, once the bankruptcy proceeding is concluded (lenders have been paid the debts due them) you are no longer liable. In legal parlance, you are "discharged" from the debts and start financially with a clean slate.

If you choose to be represented by a lawyer, remember to choose your lawyer carefully, satisfying yourself as to his or her competence, familiarity with bankruptcy law and procedure, and reputation. Bar associations and groups operated for people with distinct needs, such as the elderly or the handicapped, often operate referral services that will put you in touch with lawyers practicing in a given area of law. Recommendations from a friend, relative or acquaintance who has had a good experience with a particular lawyer may also help. And lawyer advertisements will at least make you familiar with the names of some lawyers, and some will also spell out the lawyer's area of specialization and the fee or price range for a specific type of simple case.

"The American Lawyer: When and How to Use One," another publication in the "You and the Law Series," includes information that will help you choose the best lawyer for you. (See inside front cover for ordering information.)

Remember, too, that you can, and should, discuss your lawyer's fees in advance, so that you have as clear an idea as possible of what the bankruptcy procedure will cost. Your lawyer may be paid from the assets of your estate administered by the court in the bankruptcy procedure.

Chapter 13 of the Bankruptcy Act

Chapter 13 is the most commonly used alternative within the bankruptcy code. It allows a person who has a steady income to pay all or a portion of his or her debts. Under Chapter 13, you file a bankruptcy petition and a proposed payment plan with the U.S. Bankruptcy Court. Under the rules for a Chapter 13 filing, your payments must represent all of your disposable income (whatever is not needed for shelter, food, and other necessities). Chapter 13 is available only to borrowers with less than $100,000 in unsecured debts (such as credit cards) and less than $350,000 in secured debts (such as mortgages and car loans). Anyone with greater debts generally must declare bankruptcy under Chapters 7 or 11 of the bankruptcy act. (Chapter 11 covers businesses which are restructuring while continuing operations, but a Chapter 11 filing by an individual is possible.)

Under a Chapter 13 filing, the court will distribute your proposal to the lenders, and a trustee will verify the accuracy of your petition. The court must approve your plan for it to become effective. Your proposal is likely to be acceptable if your unsecured lenders—e.g., lenders who issue credit cards, as opposed to those who make secured loans, such as mortgages—will not receive less than they would have if you had filed a straight bankruptcy petition.

A repayment plan under Chapter 13 typically extends your time for paying debts (usually up to three years or, with special permission of the court, up to five years), and may allow you to repay less than you owe. With this kind of plan you usually turn over a fixed sum of money every month to the trustee, who then pays your lenders.

Several advantages result from filing a Chapter 13 petition instead of straight bankruptcy. First, if you had people cosign any of your loans or other credit, your lenders cannot collect from your cosigners until it is clear that the Chapter 13 plan will not provide them with full payment. In contrast, if you file a straight bankruptcy petition, your lenders can immediately demand payment from your cosigners. Second, if you propose a repayment plan under Chapter 13 and successfully complete it, individual lenders cannot require you to pay them in full immediately because you gave them false financial information when you applied for the credit, or used some other fraudulent means to get credit. (However, if you partially complete a plan and the court grants you discharge anyway, you can be held liable for the full amount of fraudulent debts, even under Chapter 13.) If, on the other hand, you file for straight bankruptcy, *any* lender to whom you gave false or fraudulent information can object to discharging you from repaying the debt you owe him or her. Third, you can file under Chapter 13 more often than under Chapter 7. (The law forbids you from filing under Chapter 7 more than once every six years, but under Chapter 13 there is no prohibition against filing repeatedly.)

There may be one other advantage to using Chapter 13. When you want to reapply for credit, after your bankruptcy proceeding has concluded, potential lenders might prefer to see a Chapter 13 filing in your credit record instead of a straight Chapter 7 bankruptcy, since that option often results in your ultimately repaying your debts, or at least paying a greater percentage of your indebtedness than you might in straight bankruptcy. Lenders have no legal obligation, however, to give you any special consideration on this basis—this is something you would have to discuss with them individually when the time comes.

You should be aware, however, that there is a high failure rate in Chapter

13 bankruptcies. It is especially important to choose a competent, reputable lawyer or financial adviser to set up your repayment plan. The plan must be realistic. If you are unable to make your payments as agreed under a chapter 13 plan, you may still file for Chapter 7 (if you have not done so for six years).

An Alternative for Farmers: Chapter 12

Another option is a special type of bankruptcy which exists for farmers. Chapter 12 was added to the bankruptcy code as one of a series of special farm aid provisions enacted to help farmers survive periodic economic slumps. It allows farmers with heavy real estate debts to avoid foreclosure by pledging portions of their future crop proceeds while temporarily paying lenders the equivalent of a fair-market rent. A Chapter 12 petition may only be voluntarily filed and only by a farmer-debtor in good faith. Unless it is an expedited petition, the farmer-debtor must submit a list of lenders, as well as of assets and liabilities, and a statement of financial affairs to the U.S. Bankruptcy Court.

The farmer-debtor will in most cases require legal assistance. Any attorney representing the farmer-debtor must file a statement with the court disclosing the amount of his or her compensation.

Straight Bankruptcy: Chapter 7

Straight bankruptcy under Chapter 7 is available if less drastic methods will not solve your financial problems. Chapter 7 allows you to discharge, or extinguish, most debts. (See section below entitled "Debts You Can't Discharge" for the types of debts that you cannot avoid in any form of bankruptcy.)

Under Chapter 7, you may have to turn over many of your assets. First, when you have borrowed to buy a car, boat or other durable good, the seller may have a lien or claim on that property. If so, you may be able to keep your car, by reaffirming your debt (as explained later). If you don't reaffirm the debt, you may have to turn the property over to the lender who financed its purchase. Second, you will have to turn over all your "non-exempt" assets to the bankruptcy court to be sold for the benefit of your lenders. Non-exempt assets are those that are *not* necessary (in the eyes of the state or federal legislature) for you to have a "fresh start." Non-exempt assets include most property—land, vacation home, personal property such as jewelry or art objects, stocks and bonds and other investments, etc. In practice, however, most borrowers filing under Chapter 7 have little if any of this kind of property, but may have the kind of property—exempt property—that they can keep in bankruptcy. Exempt property includes some equity in your home (in most instances), personal items, the tools of your trade (a carpenter's tools, for example), and household furnishings of nominal value.

You cannot file for Chapter 7 bankruptcy more than once every six years. You may file a Chapter 7 bankruptcy petition on your own, but it is advisable to seek legal help when you are considering this option.

A bankruptcy proceeding begins with filing a petition with the U.S. Bankruptcy Court which contains a request that you be granted relief from your debts. As of the date the petition is filed, your assets will be subject to the protection of the court and most collection efforts against you must cease. The petition must be signed under oath; false statements could be prosecuted as perjury.

When you file the petition, you must also file a Statement of Financial Affairs, which describes your personal background and financial history.

At the same time you must also file schedules which detail your assets and your liabilities.

Under liabilites, you must include:

- your priority debts (taxes, etc.)
- your secured lenders (auto dealers, home mortgages, etc.)
- your unsecured lenders (department store credit cards, etc.)

Under assets, you must include:

- all of your real property (e.g., real estate)
- all of your personal property (household goods, clothing, cash, retirement funds, accrued net wages, etc.)
- all other assets not listed on other schedules.

You must also list all of the exemptions you are claiming. Non-exempt assets—everything except those that either state or federal law allow you to retain after your bankruptcy—will be sold to raise money to help pay off your debts. If you lie or fail to make an important disclosure, you are liable for perjury and your discharge from debts may be denied or revoked. If you make a mistake in claiming your exemptions, amendments may later be allowed to reflect the required changes.

The bankruptcy court clerk will notify your lenders that you have filed a petition, and a trustee will be appointed by the court or, in most areas, by a U.S. Trustee. Once your lenders have been notified of your petition, they must stop further efforts to collect the debts that you owe.

The trustee is responsible for examining your petition, statement of affairs and schedules, and determining what exemptions you will be allowed. It is important to note that if you disagree with the trustee's determination you can protest to the court and the court will make the final decision.

Following a determination of your exemptions the trustee will assemble and liquidate your non-exempt assets (if there are any), and first pay any "priority" claims, such as certain taxes, in full. The trustee will then pay your general unsecured lenders on a pro rata basis. If the proceeds from the sale of non-exempt assets amount to 30 percent of your debts, for example, the trustee will pay each unsecured lender 30 percent of what is due. You will then be discharged from paying any remaining balances on your general unsecured debts.

You also can reaffirm some debts, if the court approves and the lenders are willing. By reaffirming these debts, you promise to pay them in full, and you will be allowed to keep any property involved. So if you do not wish to lose property secured by a valid lien, such as a financed car or mortgaged house, you will have to continue to pay off such secured debts according to their pre-existing or renegotiated terms.

Debts You Can't Discharge

You should be aware that ten types of debt, including some tax claims, alimony, child support, most student loans and claims for punitive damages for malicious or wanton acts such as driving under the influence (DUI) are not dischargeable in bankruptcy—you will still owe and are still liable for these debts, even after you declare bankruptcy.

In Conclusion . . .

Neglecting your bills, or getting in debt over your head, or bankruptcy can affect your credit history unfavorably for many years. While there are no longer debtors prisons and your right to file for bankruptcy is protected under federal law (you can't be fired from your job, for example), you may be denied credit in the future. Remember, information in your credit file stays there for seven years and bankruptcy stays on your credit record for ten years. As long as your credit record has unfavorable information, you may have difficulty getting a new loan to buy a car on installments, or a mortgage for a new house, or a credit card.

On the other hand, declaring bankruptcy is sometimes the only reasonable alternative. Many bankruptcies are filed by people whose financial difficulties resulted from the loss of a job or as a result of a serious illness or accident. Whatever the reason, you have a legal right to file for bankruptcy. A lawyer can help you decide what is best for you.

Resources: Where Can You Get Help and More Information?

If you believe that one of the laws discussed in this booklet has been violated, you may complain to the agency charged with enforcing that law. The responsible agency is determined by the type of lender involved in the apparent violation. In the first part of this resource section you will find the major federal laws listed and the agencies responsible for enforcement of those laws. First determine the federal act that applies to your complaint; then, the type of lender with whom you have a complaint. With that information in hand, you can look up the address of the agency so that you can write to make your complaint. If you need further help, call your local consumer protection office.

The second part of this resource section deals with consumer counseling services. The third part lists various low-cost federal publications that will help you obtain and use credit effectively.

Federal Laws on Credit and Debt Collection

The *Truth in Lending Act* requires all credit grantors (banks, department stores, credit card issuers, finance companies, and so on) to provide you with the annual percentage rate (APR) of the loan.

The *Equal Credit Opportunity Act* prohibits discrimination against an applicant for credit because of age, sex, marital status, race, color, religion, national origin, or receipt of public assistance.

The *Fair Credit Billing Act* sets up a procedure for the prompt correction of errors on a credit account and prevents damage to your credit rating while you're settling a dispute.

The *Consumer Leasing Act* requires disclosure of information that helps you compare the cost and terms of one lease with another and with the cost and terms of buying on credit or with cash.

The *Fair Debt Collection Practices Act* applies to individuals and firms that regularly collect debts for others. It prohibits them from abusive collection practices and allows consumers to dispute a debt and to halt unreasonable collection activities.

WHERE TO FILE YOUR COMPLAINT

Complaints concerning consumer reporting agencies or debt collection practices should be filed with the Federal Trade Commission, as should complaints about credit issued by retail stores, department stores, small loan and finance companies, oil companies, public utility companies, state credit unions, or travel and expense credit card companies. Write:

Federal Trade Commission
Debt Collection Practices
Washington, D.C. 20580

or one of the FTC Regional Offices listed below:

Atlanta
1718 Peachtree Street, N.W.
Atlanta, Georgia 30367
(404) 347-4836

Boston
10 Causeway Street
Boston, Massachusetts 02222
(617) 565-7240

Chicago
55 East Monroe Street
Chicago, Illinois 60603
(312) 353-4423

Cleveland
118 St. Clair Avenue
Cleveland, Ohio 44114
(216) 522-4210

Dallas
8303 Elmbrook Drive
Dallas, Texas 75247
(214) 767-7050

Denver
1405 Curtis Street
Denver, Colorado 80202
(303) 844-2271

Los Angeles
11000 Wilshire Boulevard
Los Angeles, California 90024
(213) 209-7890

New York
26 Federal Plaza
New York, New York 10278
(212) 264-1207

San Francisco
901 Market Street
San Francisco, California 94103
(415) 995-5220

Seattle
915 Second Avenue
Seattle, Washington 98174
(206) 442-4655

If your complaint concerns a financial institution, the first step is to contact an officer of the institution and attempt to resolve the complaint directly.

If the financial institution has violated a banking law or regulation, the regulatory agency that oversees that category of institution might be able to help you. The following information will help you determine which agency to contact.

- National bank. If the word "national" appears in the bank's name, or the initials N.A. appear after the bank's name, write to:
  Comptroller of the Currency
  Consumers Affairs Division
  490 L'Enfant Plaza, SW
  Washington, D.C. 20219

- State-chartered bank that is a member of the Federal Reserve System, FDIC insured. Two signs will be prominently displayed on the door of the bank or in the lobby. One will say "Member, Federal Reserve System." The other will say "Deposits Insured by the Federal Deposit Insurance Corporation." For violations of federal laws, write to:
  Federal Reserve System
  Division of Consumer and Community Affairs
  20th and Constitution Avenue, NW
  Washington, D.C. 20551

or write the Federal Reserve Bank serving the area in which the state member bank is located.

Atlanta
104 Marietta Street, NW
Atlanta, Georgia 30303
(404) 586-8500

Boston
600 Atlantic Avenue
Boston, Massachusetts 02106
(617) 973-3000

Chicago
230 South LaSalle Street
P.O. Box 834
Chicago, Illinois 60690
(312) 322-5322

Cleveland
1455 East Sixth Street
P.O. Box 6387
Cleveland, Ohio 44101
(216) 241-2800

Minneapolis
250 Marquette Avenue
Minneapolis, Minnesota 55480
(612) 340-2345

New York
33 Liberty Street
New York, New York 10045
(212) 791-5000

Philadelphia
100 North Sixth Street
P.O. Box 66
Philadelphia, Pennsylvania 19105
(215) 574-6000

Richmond
100 North Ninth Street
P.O. Box 27622
Richmond, Virginia 23261
(804) 649-3611

Dallas
400 South Akard Street
Station K
Dallas, Texas 75222
(214) 651-6111

Kansas City
925 Grand Avenue
Federal Reserve Station
Kansas City, Missouri 64198
(816) 881-2000

San Francisco
400 Sansome Street
P.O. Box 7702
San Francisco, California 94120
(415) 544-2000

St. Louis
411 Locust Street
P.O. Box 442
St. Louis, Missouri 63166
(314) 444-8444

For violations of state laws, write to your state banking department.

- State-chartered bank, insured by the Federal Deposit Insurance Corporation (FDIC), but not a member of the Federal Reserve System: A sign will be prominently displayed on the door or in the lobby that says "Deposits Insured by Federal Deposit Insurance Corporation," but there will not be a sign saying "Member, Federal Reserve System." Write to:
  Federal Deposit Insurance Corporation
  Office of Bank Customer Affairs
  Washington, D.C. 20429
- Federally chartered or federally insured savings and loan association: Generally, the word "Federal" appears in the name of the savings and loan association or its name includes initials such as "FA" which indicate its status as a federal savings and loan association. A sign will be prominently displayed on the door or in the lobby that says "Deposits Insured by FSLIC." Write to:
  Federal Home Loan Bank Board
  Washington, D.C. 20552
- Federal savings bank: Generally, the word "Federal" appears in the name of the savings bank, or its name includes initials such as "FSB" which indicate its status as a federal savings bank. A sign will be prominently displayed on the door or in the lobby that says "Deposits Insured by FSLIC" or "Deposits Insured by FDIC." Write to:
  Federal Home Loan Bank Board
  Office of Community Investment
  1700 G Street, NW
  Washington, D.C. 20552
- State-chartered FSLIC insured savings institution: There will a sign prominently displayed on the door or in the lobby that says "Deposits Insured by FSLIC." The word "Federal" does not appear in the name, nor do any initials such as "FA" or "FSB." Write to:

Federal Home Loan Bank Board
Office of Community Investment
1700 G Street, NW
Washington, D.C. 20552

- State-chartered banks or savings institutions without Federal Deposit Insurance: Institution has none of the above described characteristics. For violations of federal laws, write to the Federal Trade Commission (see above). For violations of state laws, write to your state banking department.
- Federally chartered credit union: The term "Federal credit union" appears in the name of the credit union. Write to:
  National Credit Union Administration
  1776 G Street, NW
  Washington, D.C. 20456
- State-chartered, federally insured credit union: A sign will be displayed by stations or windows where deposits are accepted indicating deposits are insured by NCUA. The term "Federal Credit Union" does not appear in the name. Write to your state agency that regulates credit unions or to the Federal Trade Commission (see page 43).
- Other: If your complaint involves an institution that has none of the characteristics described, contact the appropriate state agency for violations of state laws or the Federal Trade Commission for violations of federal laws.

The FDIC maintains a toll-free Consumer Telephone Hotline to allow the public to ask questions or present views and complaints about consumer protection or civil rights matters involving FDIC-supervised banks, which include about 8,700 state-chartered banks that are not members of the Federal Reserve System. The toll-free number is (800) 424-5488. It is in daily service, Monday through Friday, from 9:00 a.m. to 4:00 p.m., Eastern Time. In the Washington, DC, area the consumer information number is (202) 898-3536. The toll-free number also reaches a telecommunication device for the deaf (TDD) and the device can be reached in the Washington area by calling (202) 898-3537.

Complaints that do not involve a violation of banking laws or regulations should be addressed first to the financial institution or other lender. If you cannot resolve the problem directly, contact your local Better Business Bureau or consumer protection office for assistance. Addresses and telephone numbers for these offices can be found in your local telephone directory, or in the *Consumer's Resource Handbook*, available free by writing to:

Handbook
Consumer Information Center
Pueblo, CO 81009

CREDIT COUNSELING

You can get credit counseling from a number of sources: credit unions, lawyers, for-profit counseling centers, to name just a few. It pays to choose your advisor carefully.

Credit counseling centers are also helpful to people having trouble paying their debts, since they contact the creditors and arrange a repayment plan. The consumer credit counseling service (CCCS) is a non-profit organization with more than 350 offices located in 47 states. CCCS counselors will help you set up a realistic budget and, on the basis of that budget, try to arrange a repayment plan that is acceptable to you and your creditors. To find an office near you, check your local phone directory for the consumer credit counseling service or write and send a self-addressed, stamped envelope to:

National Foundation for Consumer Credit Inc.
8701 Georgia Avenue
Silver Spring, MD 20910
(301) 589-5600

PUBLICATIONS

From the Federal Reserve

The following publications may be obtained without charge from:

Publications Services
Mail Stop 138
Board of Governors of the Federal Reserve System
Washington, D.C. 20551

Consumer Handbook of Credit Protection Laws (a 44-page booklet explaining how to use the credit laws to shop for credit, apply for it, keep up credit ratings, and complain about an unfair deal.)
Consumer Handbook on Adjustable Rate Mortgages
Fair Credit Billing
How to File a Consumer Complaint
If You Use a Credit Card
If You Borrow to Buy Stock
A Guide to Business Credit and the Equal Credit Opportunity Act
A Guide to Federal Reserve Regulations
Annual Percentage Rate Tables

From the Federal Trade Commission

The Federal Trade Commission publishes many popular consumer publications. They are available free by writing:

Federal Trade Commission
Public Reference
6th and Pennsylvania Avenue, N.W.
Washington, D.C. 20580

About Credit

Building a Positive Credit Record
Buying and Borrowing: Cash In On the Facts
Cosigning a Loan*
Credit and Charge Card Fraud
Credit and Older Americans
Credit Billing Blues
Credit Practices Rule*
Electronic Banking
Equal Credit Opportunity*
Fair Credit Billing*
Fair Credit Reporting
Fair Debt Collection*
Fix Your Own Credit Problems*
Lost or Stolen: Credit and ATM Cards
Scoring for Credit
Solving Credit Problems*
Utility Credit
Women and Credit Histories

About Home Financing

Escrow Accounts for Home Mortgages
Getting a Loan: Your Home as Security
Mortgage Money Guide
Refinancing Your Home
Second Mortgage Financing
Using Ads to Shop for Home Financing

About Car Financing

Car Ads: Low Interest Loans and Other Offers
A Consumer Guide to Vehicle Leasing

*Available in Spanish